# Before I Lose Light

# Before I Lose Light

S.E. Richardson

*First Edition*

Hidden Brook Press
www.HiddenBrookPress.com
writers@HiddenBrookPress.com

Copyright © 2013 Hidden Brook Press
Copyright © 2013 S.E. Richardson

All rights for poems revert to the author. All rights for book, layout and design remain with Hidden Brook Press. No part of this book may be reproduced except by a reviewer who may quote brief passages in a review. The use of any part of this publication reproduced, transmitted in any form or by any means, electronic, mechanical, photocopied, recorded or otherwise stored in a retrieval system without prior written consent of the publisher is an infringement of the copyright law.

Before I Lose Light
by S.E. Richardson

Editor – Bruce Kauffman
Cover Design – Richard M. Grove
Layout and Design – Richard M. Grove

Typeset in Garamond
Printed and bound in Canada


Library and Archives Canada Cataloguing in Publication

Richardson, S. E., 1989-, author
    Before I lose light / S.E. Richardson.

Poems.
ISBN 978-1-927725-06-1 (pbk.)

    I. Title.

PS8635.I33387B43 2013    C811'.6    C2013-906205-X

**Acknowledgements:**

This collection of poetry has been an immense privilege to write. Thank-you to Richard Grove (Tai) for taking a leap of faith in my poetry. He has offered tremendous encouragement in giving me this opportunity. Thank-you to Bruce Kauffman for his tireless editing and the weekly coffee shop visits, where he offered wisdom that was so precise in preparing me for each new week of writing woes and triumphs. For my parents- my Mom, Christie, who was an on-call, first reader and endless re-reader and for my Dad, Gord, who takes his own integrity and drive in life to my writing and my writing path; thank-you for being my closest readers and friends in this journey. My sister, Alex, for her support and inspiration as the most beautiful, truest artist I have ever known. Thank-you to my fellow writer and great friend, Christine Miscione for her understanding ear and her unfailing encouragement. Thank-you to my fellow writing comrades Stuart Ross, Carolyn Smart, Ashley- Elizabeth Best, and for my fellow Word Warriors Michael e. Casteels, Nicholas Papaxanthos & Christine Miscione; each of you inspire me in your integrity, support and your art. To everyone else for believing my poetry was worth reading. A final thank-you to my novel, Hazelnut, which has, as expressed in this collection, been a beautiful muse.

# Preface

*Before I Lose Light* is a collection of poems that leapt out of me in moments of inspiration, curiosity, a sense of play, a longing, and in times demanding my emotional strength. Found in these expressions contained within is a chord of honesty that I have tried very hard, despite the vulnerability such honesty entails, to not edit out. Please note that the first poem in this collection called "Vessels" was part of an anthology, That Not Forgotten, published by Hidden Brook Press in 2012. This poem, not only dear to my heart and a personal story, was what both led to and initiated this collection of poetry.

    I love to travel and have been lucky enough to have pursued much of it throughout my life. Many of these travels did inspire poems and ideas, as well as, a greater sense of appreciation and yearning for that place of 'home'. Once finished university and free to choose where to settle while devoting myself to my writing, I deliberately and carefully chose Kingston because of my love for the city and the eclectic writers and friends that make this city a nurturing place for my writing and, as well simply, a fun place to live. Kingston and the apartment I live in both serve and served not only as a place of home, but emerged unintentionally as a strong theme throughout this collection.

    Many of these poems also express coming to terms with the feelings I experience while facing the complex task of writing a novel that I have titled "Hazelnut". As you read through, when hearing me refer to a vast array of emotions around a thing called Hazelnut, you should know this is my novel in process. This novel has been the biggest source of inspiration I have ever yet known. The very act of creating it and trusting it enough to pursue has come from an immense treasure chest of inspiration. Even in the process of trying to write it, I am still learning about it -- figuring out what this 'thing' is, what it has to teach me about the world, about people and relationships, about myself. It is, and has been a wonderful and incredibly huge discovery.

Because a number of poems in this collection center around or come from this novel writing experience, I feel I need to elaborate just a bit on it here. From the beginning, Hazelnut has fascinated me. In fact even before as the normalcy of my life before it and then the presence of this 'new thing' after has been an interesting phenomenon for me to grapple with—where do novels come from and can you ever be ready for their arrival? Hazelnut also has, as with any novel, been a struggle to write. It is a layered and dense story that often feels a lot bigger than my own mind and intelligence can manage.

I must add that beyond these feelings that are specific to the nature of Hazelnut as a story, writing this novel has taken me to the core of experiences and feelings that most writers also go through. While there is pleasure and catharsis and imaginative journeys and discoveries and magic in the process of creating, there are also inherent challenges and struggles that writers endure—from loneliness to the feeling of impossibility and exhaustion, and to then even the worst, self-doubt.

Within this collection, most of the poems on these matters came in a cathartic form, in which the poems or verses or tidbits or whatever term one would might choose, the very use of any words to express such tough feelings became a vehicle for not only expression of but a homage to these feelings. While these feelings one has in this effort cannot (and perhaps should not) be cured nor avoided altogether, what arises with and through them can be articulated and spoken for and in this, that writing pain I was feeling can and could be better understood by my 'self' and then confronted.

As a bit of an epilogue to the sometimes trying emotions grappled with throughout much of this collection, the last few poems contained here within were poems written while on a trip with my sister, Alex, to Ireland. This was a very special trip for both of us not only because of our love for each other's company, but also the wonderful people and beautiful places in Ireland that we came upon. Ireland with its bounty of writers and the poetic voice that seems natural to its people and countryside, there, I felt a real sense of play.

This - to even just one hardworking writer out there, let it be my humble wish that just one of these poems befriend or accompany you or push you forward in those moments of struggle… as my Mother says, 'There is probably a writer in all of us'. So please take it to heart and take up that pencil and paper, and then get to it and trust and believe in yourself.

My thank you to you- the reader- who has read this far.

Sincerely,
S.E. Richardson

Contents

Preface - *p. ix*

— Vessels - *p. 1*
— Erin - *p. 4*
— The 9th Line - *p. 5*
— Travels - *p. 6*
— Lavender Glow - *p. 7*
— Noosa, Australia - *p. 8*
— South Africa - *p. 9*
— Chosen - *p. 10*
— Vision - *p. 11*
— Home - *p. 12*
— True Love - *p. 14*
— Forecast - *p. 15*
— Inner Sight - *p. 16*
— Open Mic - *p. 17*
— Wolfe - *p. 18*
— Live - *p. 19*
— Rain - *p. 20*
— The Wind of Joni Mitchell Blowing Through - *p. 21*
— Fleeting - *p. 22*
— Christy - *p. 23*
— Gore Street Apartment - *p. 24*
— Gone - *p. 25*
— My Greatest Fear - *p. 26*
— Wanting - *p. 27*
— Wanting, Revisited - *p. 28*
— Coffee & His Company. And I - *p. 29*
— Stone - *p. 33*
— My Promise - *p. 34*
— Island Man - *p. 35*
— Take Me To - *p. 36*
— Wake Up - *p. 38*
— Setting Sun - *p. 39*
— Limbo - *p. 40*
— Alone - *p. 41*

– The Story of a Novel - *p. 42*
– Contradictions - *p. 45*
– Comrades - *p. 46*
– Roadtrip - *p. 47*
– The Hope and Its Consequence - *p. 48*
– For Loreena McKennit - *p. 49*
– Wishful Thinking - *p. 50*
– Even Great Love has its Burden - *p. 51*
– Unconditional Love - *p. 52*
– Inspiration - *p. 53*
– Anticipation - *p. 54*
– Shades of Hazelnut - *p. 55*
– Pensive - *p. 60*
– The Pigeon of Victoria Station, London - *p. 61*
– A Day - *p. 62*
– Film - *p. 63*
– Lost - *p. 64*
– A Day of Sun in Ireland - *p. 65*
– Here - *p. 66*
– Alex - *p. 67*
– Foal - *p. 68*
– Dove - *p. 69*
– Motion - *p. 70*
– Missing - *p. 71*
– By the Fire's Side - *p. 72*
– Doolin Pub - *p. 73*
– Sea Breeze - *p. 74*
– Settled - *p. 75*
– Woven - *p. 76*
– The Prospect of Whitby - *p. 77*
– Alex and I - *p. 78*
– The Beginning of Every Season - *p. 81*

Author Bio Note - *p. 82*

# Vessels

Old Farm Fine Foods
Out my window
Is my coffee break.
Escaping
Kingdoms
Of articulate
Hazelnuts
Sprouting from my fingertips.

Dave
White-haired
Tough
Endearing
Generous.
Mango salsa
Organic milk
And asparagus cream cheese sandwiches.

Sydenham Public School
Stalks my sleep
Hovering over my ear
And children's laughter
Like warm breath too close
Is now my alarm.
Every morning
A father
Grey haired and balding
Holds his daughter in a hug
Hands her a purple lunch box
And waits at the fence until the bell calls her in.
His little girl
Eyes, like owl blinks
Hair like willow curtains
And her voice, high-pitched, like a caterpillar's chariot
I'd thrash my flippers while saying goodbye too.

If I walk down to Lake Ontario
With a blackboard in my hand

I don't draw the wind's travels
Or delete the wind turbines
I pause upon the Island ferry
And drive like "Aya of Yop City"
To the Credit River of Erin, Ontario
Where I once chased minnow's
Below the home of my first lover.
Feet sinking in river- bottom sand
        as thick as decomposing tree trunks.
Chalk doesn't capture the blue of his eyes
Or the wheat on his head- it's like lion's fur.
His heart, a lion.
"You're a lion," I named his heart.
"I, a deer?"
A nod
"You a deer."
So, South African accents
Carved the v's of love
That flew me to Johannesburg
Where I stood outside
The gates of his old home
Me the captive
Never to have seen the baboon that stole his biscuit.

I wanted to be an impala
        but a Canadian deer I remained.
Impala or deer
And a lion
On a beach, a desert, in a safari tent
The two are not friends
Especially not lovers.

My direction changed
Upstream the Credit River
Fuelled by 2565 canoes
Replying that I am not a minnow or a deer or an impala
I am my small town
With large blue bottles
That wait
Hopeful to fill
With underbellies
Of good decisions
And Thursdays of Professors and violin.

There were Thursdays
Professors too
But the violin
I heard the loudest in lectures
        that became my writing time.
The decision
Was made
But I had to catch up.

I am my small town
Sipping on the folk of the Grad Club.
Written on that elegant trim
Of the Victorian room
There is a historic post- script
A pleasant warning
For all writers and readers
Snowflakes
Fall like lilies
And evaporate into pink skies
Of rosy cheeks- the palettes of exhaustion
From transfusing one's poetic soul to another.

Kingston is not just my home
But a plant with many wrinkles.

And I, its photosynthesis
As I write Hazelnut
Here

        My fingertips against computer-

        My computer, a grove
        Each part an aisle
        Each page a tree.
        A word, a hazel nut.

In a cubby of Frontenac Library
On the windowpane
A single acorn
I breathe in the flamboyant fragrance
Of creative risks.

# Erin

**i.**

Canada has lakes and valleys
yellow and red leaves in the fall
and a town called Erin
that weaves with a river called the Credit.

**ii.**

We outgrew her, left her to sleep
and promised ourselves that we'd return
and recognize her every wrinkle.

But a town like Erin outgrows you.

She remakes you into a baby
left to cry in her suburbia that once was
an ocean of meadows
and horse- grazing gardens,

that landscape you feasted upon
and told your memory
she would always look like this.

**iii.**

For Julie,
Songbird sing with me
Shuffle the afternoons
Beckon our youth.

Take me to the days we rode our bikes
over the Credit on the bridge of tenth line,
drank milkshakes on Steens swivel stools,
blew out the candles that brought me
the tree house in the pines.

Where we imagined that
the gutters of our front yards
were mountain high ski hills.

Bless your father for playing along,
tying rope, where we pretended
it tugged and pulled us to its top.

# The 9th Line

In a moment
The Earth turns
It clasps your hands
And smiles at you

You accept
Carry on
The bus arrives
You depart

Hills roll
Happiness fills
Spills onto the seat next to you

A sharp turn
Where she is waiting
Sister in a knit sweater
Of chestnuts and acorns

Below trees
She is miniature
Her smile wide

You walk the country road
Side by side

Cars pass
Rocks tumble

The trees listen
Crouch closer

## Travels

In a landscape far, far more complex
Ecosystems and soil
Insects and atoms and
Life is every possible emotion
Every possible colour
Every possible detail
Every sunset
        Each unique

In this landscape you exist
With one grand leap of a life
No inscribed timeline
No whisper, 'Hurry love because you will go quick'
Your body to be earth and dust
And upon the people who loved you
       - your touch forever felt

# Lavender Glow

I like Australia in the morning the best
When the sun makes the eucalyptus pink
And the kookaburras sing

Driving
Hours and hours
Along hills and mountains
Coasts and cliffs
Beaches, their whiteness
Towns of countryside
In my seat
From the view to my imagination
       free
Moving
       like the wheels under me.

## Noosa, Australia

Sharks are present in the waves
under the moonlight.

And the eucalyptus path
to the peak over Hells Gate
        sings with kookaburras
        and sleeps with koalas.

We trace the curves of seashells
and make maps of their grooves,
wrap the pretty ones more carefully
    and tuck them
    in the secret pocket of our luggage.

## South Africa

The trees delivered leaves like letters and I pined over them, hearing the roar of lions in his stories. On the beach in Durban, he found a white shell broken into the shape of a ring and placed it on my finger. I kissed his sandy mane goodbye, rode a galloping horse without a helmet. My heartache made me daring. I trusted the horse, gave up slowing it and rolled over the Swaziland farm hills into the pink sky that held a full moon.

# Chosen

One morning in Makunduchi, Zanzibar- the air stank- the tiny bed holding my friend, Keri, and I- our mosquito net tightly strapped over us- the stars still twinkling outside the window- a grown and broken Ben came streaming into my imagination. I felt compassion for this character, this man, so sad and so shriveled. I was smitten. The rest of the story came simply by trying to understand how and why this character looked and felt the way he did that morning, every piece fell into me- Ben's story slowly exposed itself. I was an avid listener, a viewer and a landing point for his story, its womb and now its voice- I didn't choose it, it chose me. I am not writing it, it's telling me. That morning, Hazelnut was a seed just germinating, but slowly, months after her pollination in that tree of herself, the story became an intricate nut.

# Vision

I have this nut, a Hazelnut; she is a story. It is sweet and I believe, deserves telling. I see the story from beginning to end; it is intricate. I see every path that every wonderful character ventures. And I admire her, the characters, their lives each with their own fight, their own story, dreams and struggle- yet this nut remains unreachable in a hard thick shell that I cannot crack.

Maybe, if you give me a few years, allowed me that joy, to tell you its entirety, from beginning to end, its every fine detail, I can assure you: you could trust me, we would eventually arrive at its end. But in reality- it's a funny thing, a story offers only a few hundred pages at most. Don't get me wrong, I appreciate and honour this offer but to make it mine, I must break the mold that is the story, the nut, already established. It becomes necessary to rework her, shave her, thin her out, then reshape it into a captivating telling, that transports you along her beautiful country roads smoothly, with pleasure and captivation from its first page to its last. In all maybe a start in its middle, a leap ahead, then a reminisce- a subtle retrospect, a summary, sliding back to the present—enter a scene, then a dash, before I lose you. And on its way to the end, hope that this plot was crafted skillfully enough to take you along it with a smile, or a tissue or perhaps even more, in you, an uncontrollable desire to write, or to paint, or to leave that job, whatever it is that impedes your happiness. To allow you to create your own, to bloom a garden, your own garden, with every plant, flower and stem, every particle of soil and its worms in the rain. Every bird and bee and knot in the wood will be your own, however you wish them to be. It is my hope that Hazelnut will inspire.

# Home

**i.**

On that day in January
The lake paled
Branches poised like ice
The windmills gradually spun
The sky softened City Hall
       into pink
and I watched my breadth flow
behind me as I shared a smile
with a lady wearing lipstick as red as her hat.

**ii.**

Beyond the house
with its yellow door
and the three-story birdfeeder
       with a wraparound balcony
is Gore Street
       the carpet to my home.

### iii.

A birch birdfeeder
from Lake Placid
hangs from my ceiling.

It is authentic,
carved and crafted
         by someone's hands.

A wooden chest
painted blue carries
road maps of Vermont.

My laptop sits
on a coral peach foot stand,
found at the Kingston Antique Market
on a Sunday afternoon in the summer of 2012.

I sit
on a Persian carpet,
on wooden floors and write there,
basking in the sun through the bay window.

The foot stand is my desk.

Below my balcony,
in the leafless shrub,
sparrows polish their chirp.

The rads are hot to the touch
and the distant sound of an airplane
reminds me
of my wish
        for wing.

## True Love

Where the moon dips,
becoming valley
        and a forest

and a slow dancing galaxy
of birds in soft flight,

beneath a partially clad
sky of cuddling clouds

        fireflies kiss.

# Forecast

Today, I swim in the sunshine
      with words
Yesterday, I cried in the rain
      beside Bruce

Writing is weather

# Inner Sight

My idealism has deceived me, fooling me into believing that I have what it takes to chase a fleeting story and attempt to bring it to life on the page. I want encouragement. I want the best of writers, with all their talent and years of experience, with all their struggles and successes, to believe that I can do it too. I want Stephen Heighten to tell me I can to do it, to wish me to do it because Hazelnut is a story that he wants to read.

Why can't writing be as comfortable as it once was, when I raced sunrise to put nonsense on a page, oblivious to technique, dangerously passionate to simple play.

I know my characters: Ben's freckles, William's frown lines, Cecilia's hidden delicacy, Jacob in all his innocent mischief. I see them iridescently. But is this enough? I have drafted the plot, intricate and diverging. I have set the pace. Taken the greatest plunge, embraced the daunting risk: I began writing. I have accepted changes in my life, changes in myself, changes in my dreams, while Hazelnut solidified and deepened, becoming a constant. I have strengthened relationships by opening my little heart and sharing my vulnerable piece, "Yes, I am setting out to write a story." "One day a book? One day to publish?" "Maybe. But for now, I am just writing." I have built new relationships, extending myself like a growing web over a bundle of leaves—the writer within us, strings us together. I have tried with all my will to make good decisions, to write rather than talk. I have committed to my vision and with every breath in me, I chase and hope to catch, crack and manifest this story.

# Open Mic

The Artel was a cave
Its red brick
Moist cold walls

And each poet, a caveman

A timeless voice
Their each wrinkle, unique to their own
And each detail expressed,
      in the only way
their eye could have seen it

## Wolfe

The Island a delicate cocoon

The lake swells
Churning secrets

The ferry delivers
And dusk drives a red Chevy
Down the rusty gravel road

Like a bird, you curl into it
Letting the landscape draw you
Under the copper clouds
Into its nest
        a field with hay
        and blowing wheat
        and windmills
                in exact choreography

# Live

Undo the apartment
Let the clothes fall
The pages dishevel
The dishes pile
But do her back up again

# Rain

Rain has arrived
On the sunroom top
    The fire
    The wine
    The blanket

I welcome it
I welcome them

I welcome her

# The Wind of Joni Mitchell Blowing Through

Let's dance
Not because there's good music playing
But because I like you
And I like feeling your hips against mine
The blade of your shoulder at my hand
The clasp of your hand

And when I nuzzle into your neck
Would you mind if I kissed you?

## Fleeting

Though it gives me great comfort and joy to smell him on me,
I know that when his smell fades, mine will remain.

# Christy

How did my mother sound
When she read aloud
As she does now
Timeless Emerson
She as young as I am now
With the same awe
As I imagine her then
— how wise a soul
To see in her shy youth
What her soul sees now.

The reading lamp
Her face a silhouette
Her lips- the only movement
        Her voice pronounced, strong yet song
        Emerson's words move through her

All else is still
Her legs on the coffee table
Her hands, a firm hold on the book
Even her soft,
solid brunette hair at her neck

I, the daughter
Robbed
Not to see her in her youth
Blessed
To hear her now.

## Gore Street Apartment

Where I live
My steps creak
The door sticks
But doesn't slam

The tub has feet
The toilet runs
The sink plugs
      stained and slow

Bay windows
Sleep under navy skies
The kitchen reflects
Mirrors blue walls

I crawl into the glow
      of the fireplace
Curl up and sit
From there I nestle
Watch the sun settle

White trimmed walls
Paintings of Australia
A lavender, peach sunrise
Emerald pastures

Dandelions fly
Plant and grow
The street is quiet and hard
The sidewalk hums

Doors swing
Music trails
Somewhere an old man dances
To a record dusty and spinning

Take me deeper
Underneath these thoughts
Dig forever
Reach Ireland

Catch it, pass it to me
I will paint it
Offer my oil
Hang it above my bed

# Gone

The wind departs for the harbor
I wave farewell
Kindly refusing its tug

The rattle stops
The walls still
But the window is left
watching
        for its return,
and yearning
        for the trees' stroke.

## My Greatest Fear

Somewhere
On a road
Of stones
Bordered by fields
And sleeping fences

A starry sky heaves with fear
Watching a car
Blue and faded
Careening down the road
Unable to steady its swerves

That car poses
A threat to the trees
And the bushes
To the ants and to the cattle

To his neck and to his ribcage
To the blood in rivulets around his bones

And to the children, strangers
That might arrive like sudden acorns
      Tossed into his headlights

# Wanting

I wish to abandon ship.

Return to a normal life, where I can watch movies with ease, drink tea and talk about simple things, watch the sun come and go—and *Hazelnut*, her weight, her burden, her calling, her abstract abyss, her endearing and enchanting characters, her pages written, the pages unwritten, the wispy beautiful dream of her finished, tangible, and enjoyed - written and read - where I sit calm, before a sunset, in a rocking chair on a veranda, a big lake and stiff gin and tonic, with her out of me – the dream that keeps me going – I wish to erase it all, have it vanish, have her never to have appeared in the first place. I wish for simplicity, peace of mind, where I am in a woodworking shop, crafting furniture and my thoughts dash from dimensions, to stain, to colour and choice of wood, to their smell and the vision for their placement in my cozy wood home, a fire always lit, and tea always brewing, and I am safe and at ease without any of *Hazelnut* and her daring ways placed on me.

I hope I will look back upon this moment - this impossible feeling, when I have *Hazelnut* bound and coloured, its ink still wet, its first new read by virgin eyes, and I will pat this young girl's back and tell her "I knew you could do it, I knew I could do it," and to again tell myself in that day "*Hazelnut* was too stubborn of a story to allow me to quit."

And to remind myself in the here and now that – yes, *Hazelnut* **is** too stubborn a story to let me quit. I have to believe that in the end it will all be so very worth it.

## Wanting, Revisited

The pages pile, into a big pile, a heavy pile. I am not at a loss for words or stamina, but quality instead – fearing the reader would become distracted or disinterested and abandon it on any page, and the critics would feast on it, tear it apart.

That I have a story to tell, does not guarantee me the talent to tell it well. I was not handed this story along with a gift for its writing. The two did not arrive in a neat package, and I realize and I understand that one without the other can, does and will make this journey every bit self-defeating. And self-deprecating. And ever so humble.

# Coffee & His Company. And I

Dear Whimsical Wild Flower,
    My cross-legged flirt
    with Thomas Hardy
        was interrupted
    by your yellow collared shirt
    and your wave nutmeg topped.

    When I walked off the ferry
    I looked for your truck
    but found instead only an aimless island.

    Then the purple wild flowers beckoned
    and you were a mystery hiding
    a story waiting
    while I ambled, a hooded wanderer.

    When I turned around
    I saw Peter Pan chasing me
    so I stopped, keen to wait.
    Your small-talk like graceful gabble
    caught up to me.
    I hopped into your truck.
    Your graceful gabble drove us along the gravel.

    I began looking for her,
        the size of an elephant's shadow
    on the dusty windshield
    the steering wheel upside down
    on my seat belt undone.
    Giving up, I drank my American lager
    as Graceful Gabble drove us along the trail.

    Horses couldn't carry us slower
    but the engine-a fulgurous blink.

    We entered a full moon
        and I collected a meadow.
    I laid it neatly over the page
    and pleaded with the forest
    magnificent and thoughtful.
    But too soon–
    we arrived to a lawn half-cut,
    and caught a glimpse of a white-tailed deer
    in front of a cottage perched like a toad.

You had said "Blue herons are my bird",
your stories complete with paintings of them
done by past lovers.
I had forgotten my page;
      meadow abandoned
stepped inside a blue heron's nest
with the gravity of a peach.

Your cottage tasted of fudge:
rich wood, softened butter couches,
a handmade bookcase as sweet as caramelized sugar.
The stone fireplace,
      ceiling high,
enticed slackened romance.

Graceful Gabble was now an elm leaf speaking eloquently.

You handed me a pipe and I took a few puffs.
But you and her at the Juno's burnt my bliss.
That white elephant,
      she the elephant in the room,
      envious, green and famous.
My mind drifted to Athens,
a trip I'd like to take
and Eloquent Elm Leaf led me back outside.
The blue truck puttered on
      cranky with old age
driving us through the apple orchard
to a place you call "the cove".
There I saw the younger you
in a patch of cantaloupe.
And there I found again the elephant,
in the sailboat you both once shared.

We moved to the border crossing
where we crossed a taut rope
      black water rolling below.
"Well," he said "I'd really like to give you a kiss."
and we climbed to the top of the ship.

But I needed my poetry close
and with your every touch
      it silently poured out.
I longed for the forever missed lion
and his gentle blue eyes
that I couldn't find in your sea of brown.

I guess that I brought company too.

If a thread loosens
you must knit the fabric tighter.
So I ignored the harmonica
(and her strand of hair on the pillow)
        delivered
and Eloquent Elm Leaf
became a dark haired
brown-eyed
Hercules
on a Persian rug,
        naked and beautiful.

When I go back home
I don't bring my toothbrush
        from my third drawer,
I pick one at random.
But you offered me yours and
a sleep beside rippling waves.
My face flushed in the flames
when I told you of how pinecones
made for nice smelling fires.

While I slept, again the white elephant growled.
She was there in your great white house
        down the lake,
now empty.

But the early morning birds woke me
kindly tugging
while our bodies were wrapped
like a gently entwined vine.

I felt in that hug
        a lifeboat come down the river
it took the cunning you away
and left you sweet with a Spanish guitar.

I ignored the thought of all she'd sung for you
And of how you must have
strung those strings
back for her.

As the hours passed on
        your deckhand job deserted
and your boss outside threatening
you played that guitar with a tooth-full grin.

We ate ego waffles
drank lemonade
watched the rain spit and sipped black tea.
We escaped the elephants
        and all their shadows,
you and I
and your weathered chest of writing,
finally alone,
without company.

I don't doubt your kisses were real
but in your blue truck
you were once again
Graceful Gabble driving us along the gravel
and you unzipped your jacket
unbuttoned your shirt and opened your heart.

Ever so carefully you cupped the elephant
        and gave me a peek.
It was heavy and unfinished
        but your love for her
        the harmonica's voice
so beautifully golden
made me weep.
Then you rifled my innocence
        so much to make me shudder
when you said, with a cocky crooked grin,
"Poetry sessions. We'll call it that for now."

I boarded the ferry.
I told Thomas Hardy I was sorry.


Dear Whimsical Wild Flower,
    I reached Kingston and let the rain soak in.
    And in its wash, I sensed your endless façade
    and I realized, fully, my mistake of letting you in.

## Stone

Hey stone,
I see you,
I hold you,
Heavy,
Smooth,
Cold.
I want to take you for a walk
See what you're really about
Are you really as solid as you appear?

## My Promise

For the writer with the blank page,
                    silence is the muse.

Silence is

and the writing comes.

## Island Man

I felt like an apple
picked from the tree
and chewed loudly.

Sure, he chose carefully

but he chose all his apples carefully.

Like he chose his words to charm
     the details to omit,
     the details to embellish,
depending on your taste.

One day two of his favorite apples met,
they learned how greedily
he had bitten into each one of us.

He was too handsome a man
and it was too small an orchard,
for his hands to go unnoticed, unknown.

Now all the apples know,
drop and bruise
muddle up your shine

and hope all others have covered their shimmer
when he comes picking.

# Take Me To

**i.**

I want eleven nut trees
An axe for the wood
Piled for the fires
A dog for my writing days

**ii.**

Michael Casteels' boundless details
His precision and perfection
- Each chapbook, a puddle and a sky
A masterpiece
I feel his smile in each bit of its creation
When I hold their fine pages, I hold his beauty

I want the world and more for Bruce
But then, I know he has it
Out of anyone
In his smile
I see it
In abundance

**iii.**

The pointy edge of a pinecone
Between my index and thumb
The smell and the stick of sap

How wood brings me back
      to organic
      to nature
And what we're doing to it
But I am wood, I am nature, I am organic
Tainted by today's poisons

**iv.**

       Outside
       A loon call echoes off a silent lake
       To all the animals that hear it

Here
The wick and the flame

The flames dance
Something not human
But alive and thriving
Burning with me
I, otherwise alone

The flame and I
Until I blow it out

       The lily's first break through water

The dry of wet hands

The lie in bed
The covers pulled close

The dream of a cabin
Its door, I open
Meet the cool breeze, the night sky
Gravel under my feet
A lean against its wooden beams
Calm- my heart,
Everything in me, released

       All the hearts in each surgeon's hands
       Right now
       Planet wide

       Think of each heart and each hand
       That beautiful flesh in hand

## Wake Up

Let's crawl back into bed
Collapse under the wooden walls
Peak out from the red blanket
Watch Hercules clouds puff and blow on the lake

Let's climb into the clock and confuse it
Dance with its hands
Switch its numbers
Make a melody of its tick

## Setting Sun

When I threw away the last sunflower

                    I put summer away

# Limbo

Smiles, hands clasped, chatter and conversation but still, alone you are and alone you must return to your novel, alone you will finish it. Alone you go, climb into your imagination and explore and when the words don't come to describe all that you see, you may continue playing idly, or go about the world but you tread in limbo. Your smile genuine, felt, your heart in every moment, but your mind is still searching for the words and your imagination is teasing you—open and vivid, the scene tangible but out of word's reach, the silence devastates. You are without any knowing of when the words will hit, there is no forecast, no assurance that in ten seconds– or later this evening, or maybe in a week– but what if a year? Or two? You in limbo– your story begun— but your end so far, rather, your end unknown, for the middle isn't even producing- that silence kills, breaks your heart- the writer, the artist, dried up and silent, quiet and waiting- you doubt, you self-loathe, you sleep in hopes of waking up with the words, you envy students with professors to instruct them, guide them to a quarterly, the librarian to take them to the book written on that topic. A story from one's imagination is a creation, an isolated entity that you share with yourself, there's nothing before it to draw from or to add to, you cringe at the thought of every bit you've written– for nothing is as good as what you could be writing now if only the words came, you know you can do better and you will, if only you were writing. And when the words arrive, announce themselves– intrude while you are out there living, forgetting her and so very there in that moment, where is the pen and the page and the quiet desk? Quick before you lose her like the fickle wind.

## Alone

The day was cold

So cold a black cat
        dashed across Bagot Street

A chocolate lab poked his head
out of the green SUV
        and immediately retreated

Not even Pan Chancho's Moroccan salad
with its usual spicy sting on my lips could warm me.

# The Story of a Novel

Books
On my bookshelf
My coffee table
Piles on the couches
In my lap

Their print at a factory
Type pressed into each page
Ink split
Pages, quick
Stacked
One
On another
To the beat of a fast, dancing, Celtic song

The cover, the spine, the behind
Envelop- slam shut

A truck departs
Empties onto store shelves- a market
Ignore the box of the store
But think of Ireland
A few hundred years before
Where book markets were a place
for stories to be shared.

Imagine their manuscripts
That first read by the publisher
That first look by the editor's eye, discovered

I see the manuscript, formed, fully held
Like a full grown baby
In the author's hands
The moment he accepts to let it go
The placement in an envelope
A post office just isn't the writer's favourite place
Inscribing the address of the publishing house
The placement in the clerk's hand
The wish to grab it back
"No! How dare you take it!"
The walk away
Leave it

Let it go
The slam of the post office door
Then in my lap, another's book
I see in it its once incomplete and scattered sentences
But the idea within it, the spark there
The edits to bring it to full flame

I see the writer's mind in pursuit
Viewing their imagination
The delivery of all they see
Both in imagery and analytically
Mining away at a deeper point to be made
The correct and exact combination of words
To tell it all

I feel the author's initial joy
In the wonderful bit I just read
And in the sadness

I feel their sadness
How they were experiencing it when they wrote it
I wish I could have been there
Given them a hug
Them alone with it for so many years
Until its finish and their share,
        until their sadness shared

I see the author's story in them
This story they want to tell
I see them on the sidewalk
Walking to the grocery store
Absent, but not,
        they, simply thinking of their story

I see her defending her need to write it
To her husband
Missing her, or loving it, still he grows tired,
Impatient for its end
Looses faith it will ever finish
To his now ex- boss
        *'but this story is urgent and important'*
His boss
        *'Worth loosing your job over?!'*

Her father
>	supportive and loving


Her mother
>	always there, from the beginning

I see all the people who encouraged her
Took the leap with her and believed in her

I see the formation of the characters
The joy when meeting, viewing them all for the first time

I see their first journeys
>	along their roads
>	into their forest

Through their houses
The socks inside their drawers
The spices in their kitchen cupboards
Their wardrobe inside their closet

The carpet on their floor
The paintings on the wall
The size and shape of their windows
The scent and colour of the room

I see their first day
>	that first second
In this
>	their discovery of their story

## Contradictions

The lie:

that I am in my third year
of writing *Hazelnut*
means nothing.


The truth:

I have truly
enjoyed every minute.

## Comrades

At least Thomas Hardy,
As lonely as I am now,

       sits nearby on the bookshelf.

# Roadtrip

My Mother and I,
        two raindrops in simultaneous fall
Wheeling over back roads to Lake Placid
Eyes open for moose
The Adirondacks in fall leaf

We entered *Hazelnut*
I the pen
Her the paper
        In the car, each hotel room, each and every meal,
        Her careful ear
        Absorbing the scenes
        Creating them with me
        Together, searching for just the right dialogue
        Sequencing the plot

        When to narrate, not to show
        When to show, not to narrate
        We found Hazelnut inspirations everywhere

And Vermont was a home
We nestled into
Carved love notes
Into its winding roads
And unleashed our dreams
To meet again one day
Our imaginations were two horses
Galloping side by side
Travelling great distances

On the peak of each mountain
I saw my story's finish
The climb long and strenuous
But the vista long and clear
My mother, the wise one
My ear begged for more
And with her every laugh
Life shed a heavy coat

## The Hope and Its Consequence

And then when you are writing
You are writing
The emails go unanswered
The phone rings

But you are writing
Fully here in that world
And nothing else matters

# For Loreena McKennit

We are driving but
We are not driving
We are riding
(The highway)
Our wheels
        hooves
Galloping

## Wishful Thinking

If *Hazelnut* were a series of rooms
Each room held the scene
And I had the map, a directory

The rooms titled and numbered
I could step into each room
Observe the scene on replay
Tweak it, become it, negotiate with my characters

And the rooms were in a large house
Nothing like a building or an institution
But a big wooden house, its walls, beautiful
And the house, in Vermont
Where I step out into mountains
By a river
Cool air

In the house, at the center
Or maybe a level above
Where the rooms had no roofs
I could watch each scene
Puppet and control

There, a large desk
A pen, a page,
The scribble becoming immediately typed
Punctuated and contemplated
In the fireplace, tossed away words- edits
Swept and burnt, blown away
Maybe to catch again another day

And then the pages of my book
Typed, beautiful and bound
Emerge, complete, into a pile beside me.

## Even Great Love has its Burden

I am crushing under Hazelnut. The weight of Hazelnut is upon me and I'm collapsing, I can't bear such a big story.

## Unconditional Love

I'll take you Vermont
In your green, red or yellow leaf
In your road
        snowy or paved
        winding or flat
In your deer, your ever-moving tractors
In your antique shops
Cider factories
In your grand vistas and your little bends
In your friend New York
        and its Lake Placid

# Inspiration

In the car,
on the way back
      from Burlington-

my hand racing to write
before I lose light

# Anticipation

The twig looks frail
        bendable
at the mouth of a river

The clouds murmur hurried sentences
of oncoming snowfalls

Flocks of birds carry keys
on their wings to ceaseless summers

The sun hangs loosely on dried flowers
Dawn searches for longer days

The eye of winter distorts

The flies half-lift their tired heads
        to illusions of daisy field meadows

# Shades of Hazelnut

**i.**

I'm the Peter Pan who wants to live in Hazelnut forever.
I don't want to finish writing it.
I don't want Hazelnut to end.
I felt completely blindsided,
felt betrayed to realize it has an end.

I, for so long at the beginning or
somewhere deep in the middle,
dwelling there in its cozy arms
and the many blankets
        and runs
        and dances
        and tears I found there.
I hadn't really thought of it ending
or of my life without it and all its characters.

The realization hit me like tsunami grief,
landing me in devastating weeps.

If only I had thought a little further ahead,
kept its end in sight
so to remind myself of our ultimate parting,
        to protect myself from its brevity.

**ii.**

Though these characters are fictional,
it's like coming to an end of a journey
with some really good friends and
        saying goodbye forever,
        parting for life.

They have come to feel so real,
each their own entity
each in their own entirety.

I have gotten to know
and have fallen in love with each one,

my heart breaks to let them go.

**iii.**

My typewriter is playful
A periwinkle blue
A soft lilac

She is devout
Punctual, prompt

She tidies trees into neatly dictated letters
Plucks the noisy words for me
Ripens each sentence into distinct suns

Most keys are buoyant
Though some cling,
       Slowly release

If she had feet or wings or wheels
She'd follow me around my day
Cleverly tucking herself out of sight

Once I saw her in a fury
Heard quick strokes of her keys
All on her own
She had delivered me a page
Imagine my astonishment
As I read from her imagination
Of a fleeting romance
Over the course of a half century.


Out of the ground
Sturdy tall limbs
Branches
A bud
Like two hands
Holding a fetus
Opens soft green leaves

*She wore brown loafers*
*That had walked the fields of Avignon*

*She loved sunflowers, language,*
*the sound of a dry leaf blowing on the sidewalk*

*She tilted her head*
*In awe of the light on the frost on her window*

*Her auburn hair lent her eyes its pigment*

*Her shoulders were as delicate as her hand print*

*She rests pieces of wood by her fireplace solely to admire*

*Her desk is a lyrical poem*

*She burns a candle that sits beside her bed*
*Like a butterfly perched on a petal*

**iv.**

Oh willow, oh willow
How sweet your tress
In the wind blow

And the stillness
In the sway
Of the bulrushes below

## Pensive

The top of tall scraggly pines,
my destination.

The grip of their proud warm limbs,
where only in their highest, wind- swept needles
the eagles nest.

Their eyes watching my waitressing steps,
their claws clenched, their breath held
and their feathers squeezed
        hunting my writing for real poetry.

# The Pigeon of Victoria Station, London

Through her glowing instinctive eyes:
A sea of hurried legs,
wheels of trains departing,
her feet pressed against cold cement
ever ready to move
in a dance of defense against the shuffling.

## A Day

The cliffs brew castles.
Narrated by Ogma.

The flesh of a mare
gallops a bristled meadow
as the sun bronzes her chestnut fur.

She rests under the apple tree,
grazes the green carpet for fallen fruit,
gallops the length of the meadow once more
and settles in the paddock
its bucket of oats,
        waiting for the beauty
        of another day.

# Film

You were photographed
lips parted at dawn,
on a short wooden stool
in a smoky small stone room
under a thatched roof,
in that thin lace of a dress.

The point was to flaunt your intelligent eyes
at the end of a long dirt road
writing thunderous words
upon old stained paper.

And he, beyond the lens,

>an eclipse of glass
>on charcoal slate,

>a grown man
>like a pearly angelic child.

# Lost

Her eyes hung solemnly
on the picture.

We tried to pass the time
driving the hills
        edging the stony ridge.

Sunrise crawling through the garden,
        dipping even the weeds in gold.

Blotched in the valley below,
the cattle
        an inky brown.
And still, her fingers grasped
at the edges of the photograph:
        his blunt jaw,
        his eyes opaque,
        that halo of dusted sun around him
        an easy smile captured
        and his callused hands.

But still, the lens
couldn't peel off the uniform
        as she had lovingly over their years.

# A Day of Sun in Ireland

On the fourth sunny day in Ireland.

Tired sheep curled up
beside narrow winding roads.
A picnic table in the sun
outside the smokehouse.

Celtic crosses nested into
the hay like grass.

A field of sapphires
shaken and tossed.

And at the cliff's edge,
the sun is
making glass marbles of the water .

# Here

Above a laundry bin
a clothesline of sheets
        is blowing gaily in the wind.

This page is my basket,
a collector of images.

And I realize for the first time
I am here
I am here
I am here and
I am not just a traveler.

# Alex

With a polite gaze
she takes in the horizon.

Body stern against the sun,
freckles are taking hold of her face.

Sitting so gracefully atop its back,
her knit sweater like cauliflower soup,
she takes hold of the reins like a knowing rider.

## Foal

Before the cliffs and the sea and the narrow winding roads,
in a century old barn, strewn with dust and mould and holes
and webs and mice and broken down stones,
      at the top of a grassy hill over the Atlantic
      on the West Coast of Ireland,
the town of Doolin lays awake
listening
      to the nearby cry of a mare's agonizing moans.

Her mane sweaty in his fingers,
her strained head,
her belching black eyes
      in the hay.

Dank in the smell of birthing,
      his tweed vest and dark jeans,
      his tall brown boots
drenched in cold sweat and wet of blood.

Seconds passing like hours.
His knees numb from kneeling,
      his breath heavy over the morning air.

With one last push,
      the vet's keen nod,
the barn closes her eyes and
the mare willing
      with all life in her,
births a foal.

The news comes to us
in the middle of the night,
as we are left in joyous tears
by Peter's noble words
      "I'll name her after you, Alex."

# Dove

From a lidless wooden box
he lifts her.

The white bird, her gypsy wings,
Sinking into the bowl of his hand.

His palm under her warm belly,
her claws clasp, pierce his tough skin.

Her feathers glow, a sunlit cloud.
Her heartbeat resists the tip of his index finger.

She trusts him.

He gently places her by the dusty grey barn,
shaded from the sun,

undoes the button of his collar,
collapses beside her in the tousled, ripened wheat.

# Motion

My beer glass has dancing feet.
The stool legs are shyer,
        shuffling one to the other.
Woolen caps lift and lower.
Even the white stucco houses
come tumbling down the hill,
        pebbles,
their chimneys leaving trails
like silent and vanishing jets in the sky.

# Missing

She wanted to be hearty like the seagull surfing the wind,
in the cove of the cliffs.
The waves were merciless
against the sharp shard of the charcoal rocks.
She longed for her betrothed's temple,
      tucked safely on her chest.

Their daughter played steps on the stones beside her.
Gay and distracted like the tumbling playful waves.
At night while the copper kettle whistled,
and she undid her mother's tight bun
letting her brunette curls fall to her waist,
she cried for her father too.

Emily was conceived right there where she sat,
while the hay blew and the dry bush rustled.
They had waited years,
for his love to ripen into a loyal boulder,
like the ones of the stone fence that lined
and rivered down the countryside.

When she was kissed by him
she was kissed by the Irish Sea.

## By the Fire's Side

The hospitable Doolin Hostle
      at the Cliffs of Moher,
where the white horse waits,
galloping to greet, playful,
but still patient at the fence.

The scone.

The soup.

The soda bread.

The sunset over the Atlantic,
      castle praline grey.

All ladders to the sun.

# Doolin Pub

The tea light flickers shadowy figures on the wooden table.
Its wrought iron legs were about to take off on us
if we didn't read our poetry louder.
Listening, the wood's fine amber grain winked at us,
and the stone archways humbly hunched over.
The fire stopped its crackle, as the lanterns alerted
all others and sent the leprechauns
        the little ones
as ears.

## Sea Breeze

Above the cobblestone
        chattering at walker's heels and loafers,
beneath the smoke rising from a chimney'd pub
        and its scent filling the street,

here at twilight,
Galway's seagulls speak.

## Settled

I could unpack my luggage in that apartment
Let the closet attach locks to my clothes
And throw away the key

The walls always pleaded for more
        paintings or photographs
Listening keenly
Leaning in closer
        to all the stories of where I had been.

# Woven

The travels of an ant

The web of a spider

The drip of pine sap

Journeys of a dragonfly

The cup of a leaf

Nature
        its narrative finely crafted
holds stories
        woven and infinite

# The Prospect of Whitby

Deep in the heart of Wapping
in the London Borough of Tower of Hamlets,
the Prospect of Whitby rests,
      the oldest pub on the Thames.
There I'd never tire,
with a pint by the fire,
of the Prospect of Whitby.

Its dark wood garnish,
displayed ship relics,
the pewter-topped bar
with wheels and lanterns.
Avaste ye, Heave ho,
ropes dangling from the beams and
steel –toed boots clank on the flagstone floors
Heave ho, aye, Heave ho.

Once, "Hanging Judge Jeffery's"
watched the noose take the pirates
      as he dined.
I'd like to think
"Hanging Judge Jeffery's"
was a man of justice, not hatred.

Here deep in the heart of
this town of Wapping and
of the Prospect of Whitby,

      I'd never tire.

# Alex and I

i.

Alex and I
On a train to Wales
With *The Great Gatsby*
and Frank O'Connor's *The Mad Lomasney's*

She in soft blue
I in plaid
Lost in covers
O'Connor is Father MacEnerney's Church
     by a bridge over a basin
Fitzgerald is black and white
     tall pines, their tall thin trunks visible
     the old black car, its giant wheels
     its giant headlights and
     a lady's smiling face from the driver's seat

Outside
We pass a flock of thick furry lambs
Black hooves
Black ankles
The rest of their bodies, a muddy cream
Stout and watching back
Close to the grass

The sun breaks free
Revealing the window's water stains
My gaze tightens to the sun
I can't help the frown on my brow
I tuck my hair behind my left ear

Under that same sunlight –

The slender red brick homes
Black shilling roofs
Their thin tall chimneys

Dry green hedges

With their 90 degree corners
Help to define

Vultures fly and swoop
The brittle meadow
Barren like a buzz cut

Some ponds float the swans
Others are empty,
With but the dull reflected sky

Crewe South Junction
Its peeling pastel salmon paint
Train tracks
Stones
Pigeons
Telephone wires
Mustard yellow brick
Behind decorative arches

Snow dusts the hill of England in April
I brought Dinesen's
*Out of Africa*
And *The Way to Come Home*
By Carolyn Smart

ii.

Cheshire Station and the herd of police
        with their tall black velvet hats
Under the hanging planter
        of light pink peonies and green leaf
The grandfather reaching for his granddaughter's hand
85 Miles to Holyhead
Noisy men stepping on the train
Disrupting
Making the lady with the glasses at the end of her nose
Turn her head and scoff
They collect by the snack cart
Drink beer and flirt with the cart lady
Their slow rise of laughter and burly voices
Making the lady's head swivel
        with eyebrows raised in disapproval
Alex disappears behind the electronic doors
Visits the snack cart with the lady and her friendly British accent
We pass race tracks
Many white tents
Holding crowds of people
Passengers rise a little off their seats
Straining their necks to catch a dash of horses

Alex returns with a Walkers Pure Butter Shortbread Cookie
Its plaid wrapper matches my jacket
We share our headphones
Together listening to Johnny Clegg's *Didi*
The couple we face
Politely pretend not to notice the shortbread crumbs
        covering my black turtleneck like chalk

We switch to Lightfoot's *I'm Not Saying*
And together write a poem
I feel pregnant with ideas, stories
I've been graced by the sight of lamb
A small, delicate, white lamb
By the stone walls
By the sea

# The Beginning of Every Season

The beginning of every season
Holds promise for me
I calculate the new moons
Schedule the rainy days
Sweep some sun into a jar
Place it in my cupboard
Between the sugar and the coffee
And the granola that I love
I sailboat across my living room
Anchor myself to my desk
Throw a fire onto the page
Ready words piled beside me
Pick up my landline
Dial the future
And ask

    if my novel will really be finished by May.

# Author Bio Notes

**S.E. (Sarah Elizabeth) Richardson** is originally from the town of Erin, Ontario. Sarah grew up in the presence of pine trees and many indoor and outdoor fires. Sarah loved growing up in a small town where she spent much of her time outdoors, exploring the valleys and hills around her home and venturing through the many disused trails leading to the Credit River. In these times, she felt her imagination was fostered, and she was free to daydream.

Throughout her childhood, Sarah traveled and lived in Australia several times and has visited countries such as, New Zealand, Thailand, Hong Kong, South Africa, Mexico, Tahiti, Fiji and has ventured throughout Europe. Sarah enjoys road trips for their sense of adventure, movement and time for imagination.

Sarah completed an undergraduate degree at Queen's University in the field of International Development Studies. This degree included an internship in her fourth year of study, where in 2010, she lived and volunteered in a small town called Makunduchi, on Zanzibar Island off the coast of Tanzania. This was a pivotal experience in her life-- witnessing profound joy and love despite material deprivation led to a wider appreciation for complexity and diversity in cultures and human experience. While there she found an ever-renewing value for life and the need to follow one's dreams, which gave her the strength and faith to prioritize the thing she loves most, writing.

While at Queens University, Sarah benefited greatly from Carolyn Smart's creative writing course, as well as, the writer-in-residence position that held poet and fiction writer Stuart Ross, in 2010, as a mentor and reader for the Queen's and Kingston community. Working with Stuart Ross on her writing was hugely influential on her integrity and on her experience as a writer. Sarah also feels very privileged for the support and reading by Diane Schoemperlen, who was writer-in-residence in 2012. Sarah is also part of a writing group called Word Warriors, and workshops her poetry and fiction with respected poet, Ashley-Elizabeth Best. Early in 2013, Sarah became a member of the Canadian Cuban Literary Alliance. Sarah Richardson has been published in 529 (Proper Tales Press), That Not Forgotten (Hidden Brook Press), illiterature - issue two (Puddles of Sky Press), Inspired Heart (Melinda Cochrane International), and is currently writing two novels. When Sarah is not writing poetry or working on her fiction, she is likely reading or doing yoga, or can be found in downtown Kingston serving either delicious Pad Thais or artful lattes. After work, Sarah often races down to the lakeside to catch the setting sun.

# Books in the North Shore Series
Find full information at
– http://www.HiddenBrookPress.com/b-NShore.html

## 2 Anthologies

***Changing Ways*** is a book of prose by Cobourg area authors including: Jean Edgar Benitz, Patricia Calder, Fran O'Hara Campbell, Leonard D'Agostino, Shane Joseph, Brian Mullally. Editor: Jacob Hogeterp
— Prose – ISBN – 978-1-897475-22-5

***That Not Forgotten*** - Editor – Bruce Kauffman with 118 authors from the North Shore geographic area.
— Prose and Poetry – ISBN – 978-1-897475-89-8

### First set of five books

— M.E. Csamer – Kingston – *A Month Without Snow*
  – Prose – ISBN – 978-1-897475-87-2
— Elizabeth Greene – Kingston – *The Iron Shoes*
  – Poetry – ISBN – 978-1-897475-76-6
— Richard Grove – Brighton – *A Family Reunion*
  – Prose – ISBN – 978-1-897475-90-2
— R.D. Roy – Trenton – *A Pre emptive Kindness*
  – Prose – ISBN – 978-1-897475-80-3
— Eric Winter – Cobourg – *The Man In The Hat*
  – Poetry – ISBN – 978-1-897475-77-3

### Second set of five books

— Janet Richards – Belleville – *Glass Skin*
  – Poetry – ISBN – 978-1-897475-01-0
— R.D. Roy – Trenton – *Three Cities*
  – Poetry – ISBN – 978-1-897475-96-4
— Wayne Schlepp – Cobourg – *The Darker Edges of the Sky*
  – Poetry – ISBN – 978-1-897475-99-5
— Benjamin Sheedy – Kingston – *A Centre in Which They Breed*
  – Poetry – ISBN – 978-1-897475-98-8
— Patricia Stone – Peterborough – *All Things Considered*
  – Prose – ISBN – 978-1-897475-04-1

**Third set of five books**

— Mark Clement – Cobourg – *Island In the Shadow*
  – Poetry – ISBN – 978-1-897475-08-9
— Anthony Donnelly – Brighton – *Fishbowl Fridays*
  – Prose – ISBN – 978-1-897475-02-7
— Chris Faiers – Marmora – *ZenRiver Poems & Haibun*
  – Poetry – ISBN – 978-1-897475-25-6
— Shane Joseph – Cobourg – *Fringe Dwellers* Second Edition
  – Prose – ISBN – 978-1-897475-44-7
— Deborah Panko – Cobourg – *Somewhat Elsewhere*
  – Poetry – ISBN – 978-1-897475-13-3

**Forth set of five books**

— Diane Dawber – Bath – *Driving, Braking and Getting out to Walk*
  – Poetry – ISBN – 978-1-897475-40-9
— Patrick Gray – Port Hope – *This Grace of Light*
  – Poetry – ISBN – 978-1-897475-34-8
— John Pigeau – Kingston – *The Nothing Waltz*
  – Prose – ISBN – 978-1-897475-37-9
— Mike Johnston – Cobourg – *Reflections Around the Sun*
  – Poetry – ISBN – 978-1-897475-38-6
— Kathryn MacDonald – Shannonville – *Calla & Édourd*
  – Prose – ISBN – 978-1-897475-39-3

**Fifth set of three books**

— Tara Kainer – Kingston – *When I Think On Your Lives*
  – Poetry– ISBN – 978-1-897475-68-3
— Morgan Wade – Kingston – *The Last Stoic*
  – Novel – ISBN – 978-1-897475-63-8
— Kathryn MacDonald – Shannonville – *A Breeze You Whisper*
  – Poetry – ISBN – 978-1-897475-66-9

**Sixth set of three books**

— Bruce Kauffman – Kingston – *The Texture of Days, in Ash and Leaf*
  – Poetry – ISBN - 978-1-897475-86-7
— Chris Faiers – Marmora – *Eel Pie Island Dharma: A hippie memoir/haibun*
  – A memoir in haibun form – ISBN - 978-1-897475-92-8
— Theodore Michael Christou – Kingston – *an overbearing eye*
  – Poety – ISBN – 978-1-897475-93-5

**Seventh set of four books**

— Alyssa Cooper – Kingston – *Cold Breath of Life*
  – Poetry – ISBN – 978-1-927725-02-3
— Bruce Kauffman – Kingston – *The Silence Before the Whisper Comes*
  – Poetry – ISBN – 978-1-897475-98-0
— S.E. Richardson – Kingston – *Before I Lose Light*
  – Poetry – ISBN – 978-1-927725-05-4
— G. W. Rasberry – Kingston – *More Naked Than Ever*
  – Poetry – ISBN – 978-1-927725-04-7

www.ingramcontent.com/pod-product-compliance
Lightning Source LLC
Chambersburg PA
CBHW060501080526
**44584CB00015B/1507**